I is for Imagination!

224 Coloring and Activity Pages

Bendon Publishing International, Inc.
Ashland, OH 44805
www.bendonpub.com

SESAME STREET

Which picture is different? Circle it.

1.

2.

3.

4.

Can You COLOR the OBJECT?

COLOR the SMALLEST pear in the box GREEN!

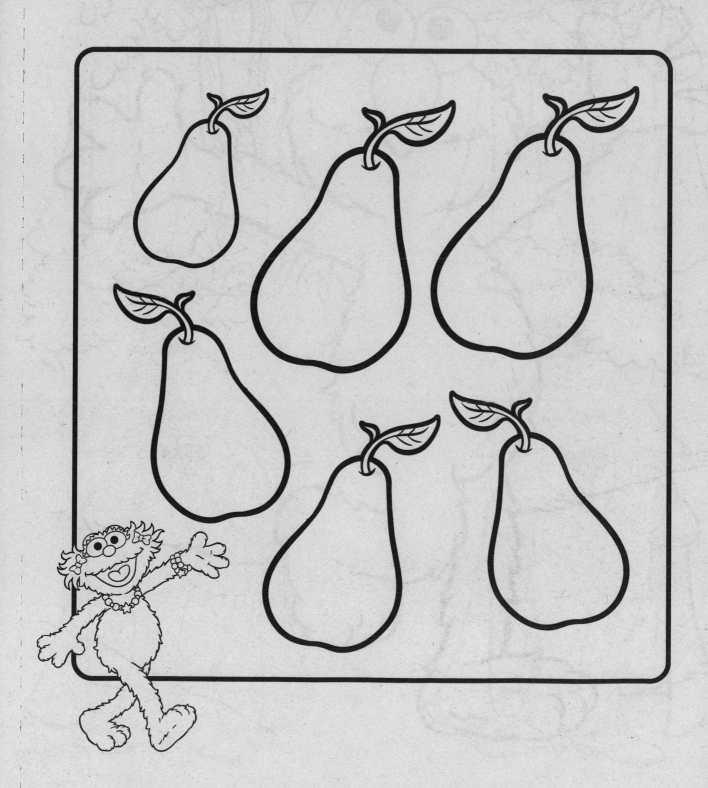

Help the friends find a way to each other.

Draw a picture of your best friend.

Draw lines connecting the pictures that match.

Draw lines connecting the pictures that match.

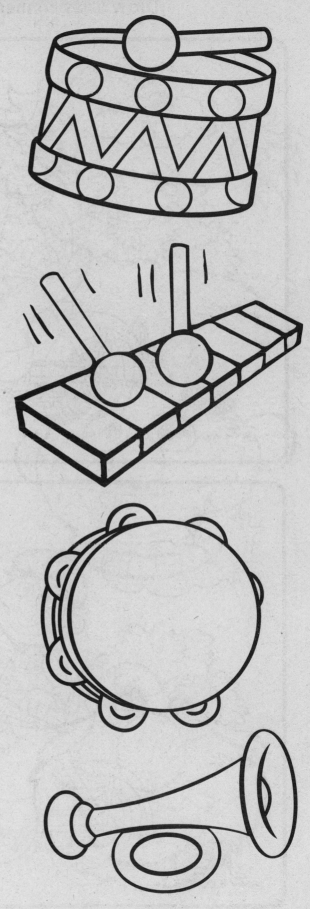

Find two things that have been added to the picture on the bottom. Circle them.

Draw a picture of your favorite bird.

Draw Bert by following the numbered pictures. Bert loves his pet pigeon, Bernice. Draw Bert with Bernice.

1.

2.

3.

Draw lines connecting each character to their favorite toy or pet.

Draw lines connecting the shapes that match.

Count the bats. Circle the correct number.

2 3 4 5 6

Draw a dog by following the numbered pictures. Color the dog any color you like. Draw a bone for him to chew on.

1.

2.

3.

Help Bert find a way through the maze to Ernie.

Start

Finish

1	2	3	4	5	6	7	8	9	10
red	blue	green	yellow	orange	brown	black	pink	purple	gray

Take Elmo through the maze to Oscar.

1	2	3	4	5	6	7	8	9	10
red	blue	green	yellow	orange	brown	black	pink	purple	gray

Find a way through the maze.

Start

Finish

Count the crayons in the frame.

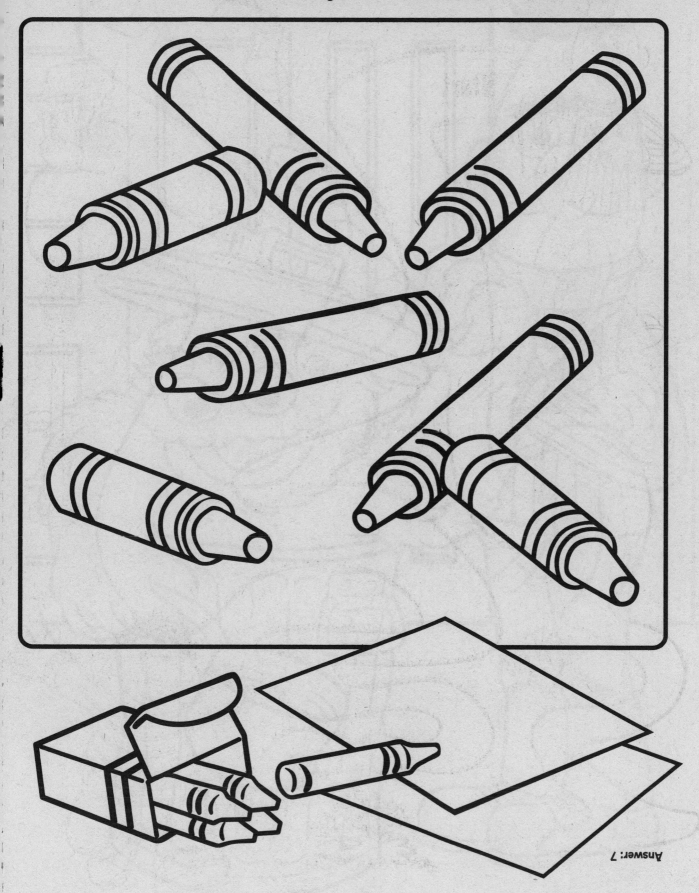

Answer: 7

Draw lines connecting the pictures that match.

Draw Cookie Monster by following the numbered pictures.

1.

2.

3.

1	2	3	4	5	6	7	8	9	10
red	blue	green	yellow	orange	brown	black	pink	purple	gray

Find the triangle. △ Color it green.

Find the circle. ○ Color it red.

Find the square. □ Color it blue.

Find the star. ☆ Color it yellow.

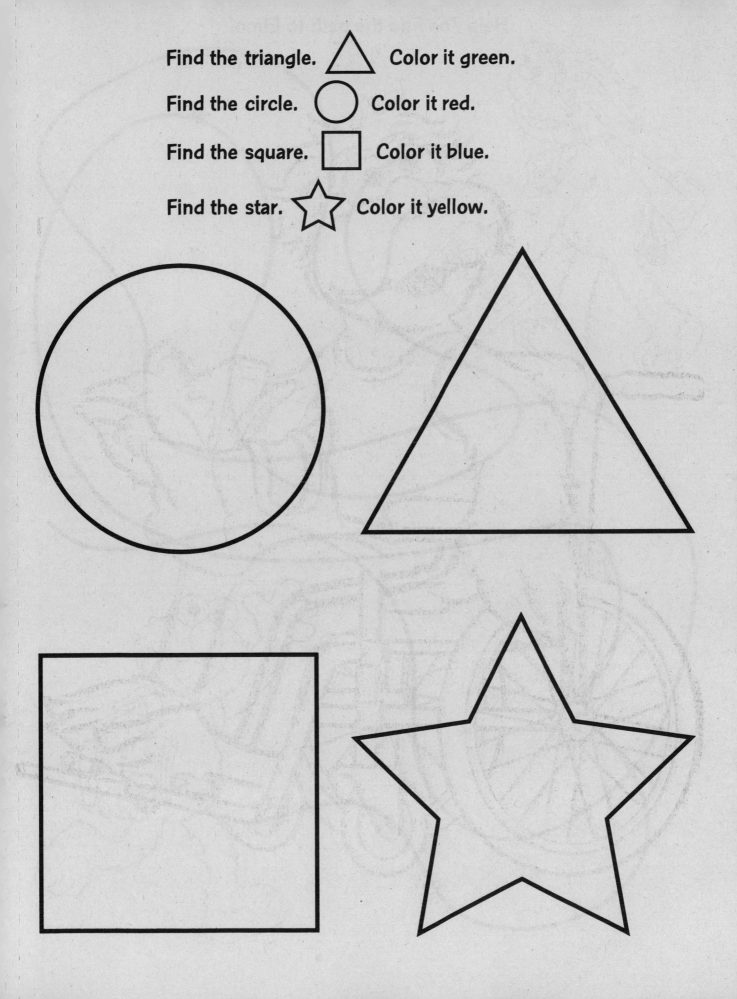

Help Zoe find the path to Elmo.

1	2	3	4	5	6	7	8	9	10
red	blue	green	yellow	orange	brown	black	pink	purple	gray

Take Zoe to 123 Sesame Street

Find two things that have been added to the picture on the bottom. Circle them.

Find the path that connects the two friends.

Draw Elmo by following the numbered pictures.

1.

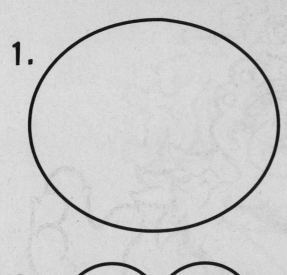

2.

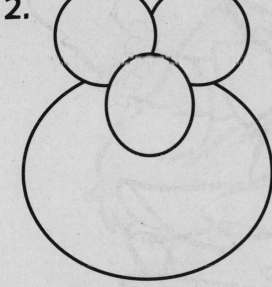

3.

1	2	3	4	5	6	7	8	9	10
red	blue	green	yellow	orange	brown	black	pink	purple	gray

1	2	3	4	5	6	7	8	9	10
red	blue	green	yellow	orange	brown	black	pink	purple	gray

Draw lines connecting the pictures that match.

You can draw!
Copy the picture square by
square in the grid below.

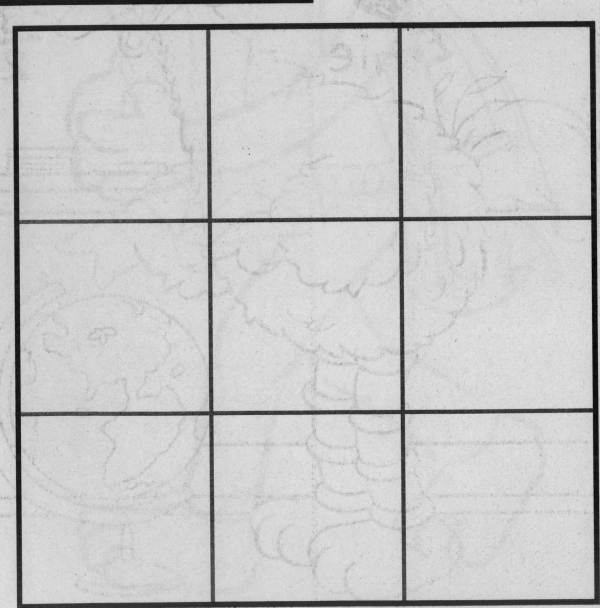

1	2	3	4	5	6	7	8	9	10
red	blue	green	yellow	orange	brown	black	pink	purple	gray

Which picture is different? Circle it.

1.

2.

3.

4.

Which picture is different? Circle it.

1.

2.

3.

4.

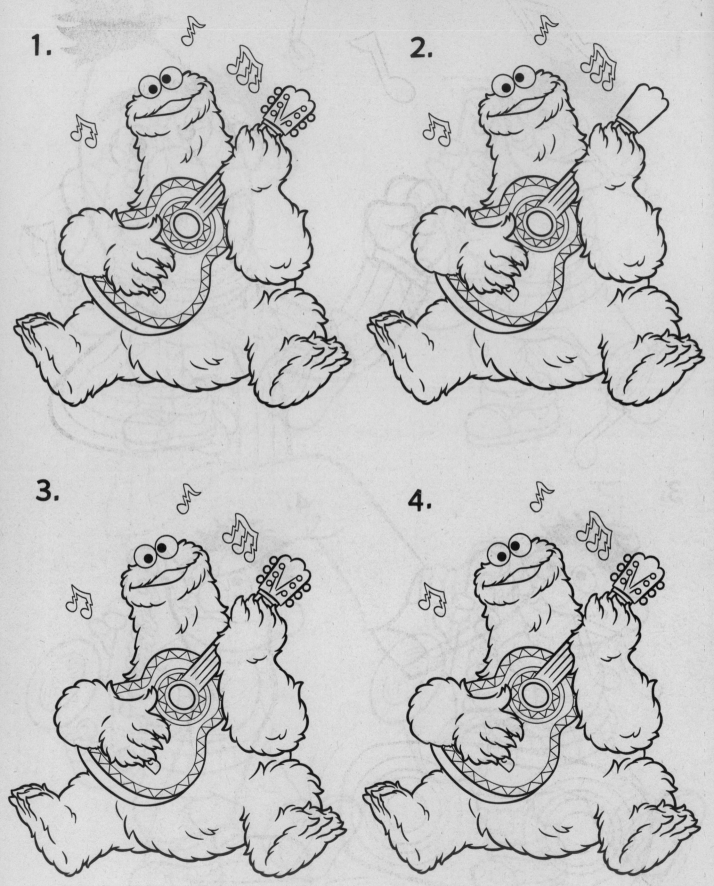

1	2	3	4	5	6	7	8	9	10
red	blue	green	yellow	orange	brown	black	pink	purple	gray

Draw Zoe by following the numbered pictures.

1.

2.

3.

Draw lines connecting the pictures that match.

HOW MANY CAN YOU COUNT?

Count the number of chicken legs in the box!

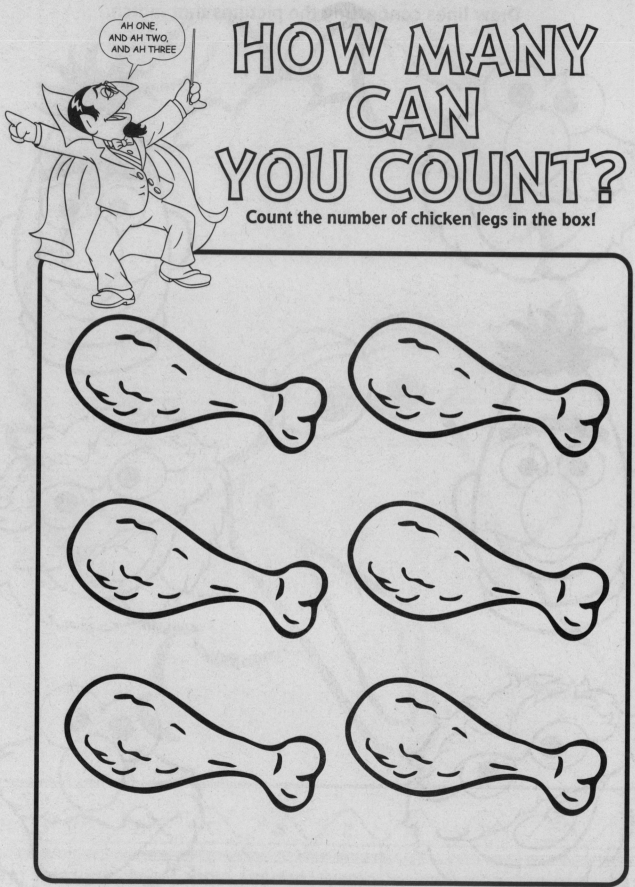

1	2	3	4	5	6	7	8	9	10
red	blue	green	yellow	orange	brown	black	pink	purple	gray

COUNT and COLOR

COUNT how many watermelons are in the box below. THEN COLOR each each watermelon RED and GREEN!

COUNT and COLOR

COUNT how many strawberries are in the box below. THEN COLOR each strawberry either PINK or RED!

answer: 12 strawberries

1	2	3	4	5	6	7	8	9	10
red	blue	green	yellow	orange	brown	black	pink	purple	gray

Draw lines between the pictures that match.

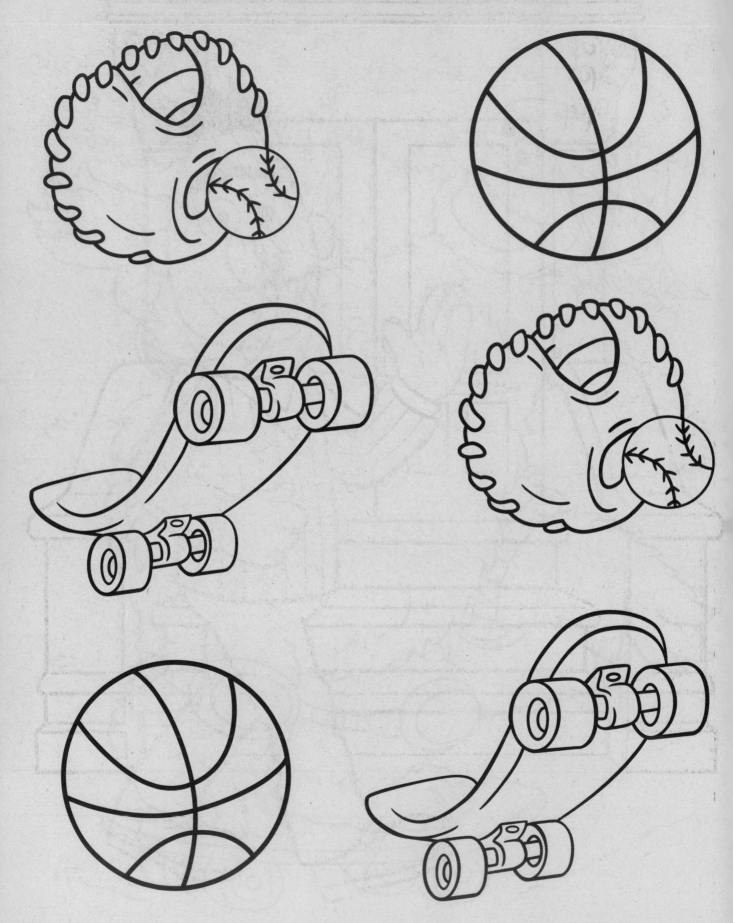

Can You COLOR the OBJECT?

COLOR the LARGEST cookie in the box BROWN!

1	2	3	4	5	6	7	8	9	10
red	blue	green	yellow	orange	brown	black	pink	purple	gray

1	2	3	4	5	6	7	8	9	10
red	blue	green	yellow	orange	brown	black	pink	purple	gray

HAVE FUN DRAWING!

DRAW and COLOR a picture of your favorite SPRINGTIME SNACK !

Can You COLOR the OBJECT?

COLOR the SMALLEST bundle of grapes in the box PURPLE!

1	2	3	4	5	6	7	8	9	10
red	blue	green	yellow	orange	brown	black	pink	purple	gray

AH ONE, AND AH TWO, AND AH THREE

HOW MANY CAN YOU COUNT?

Count the number of oranges in the box!

Count the bats.

Draw lines between the pictures that match.

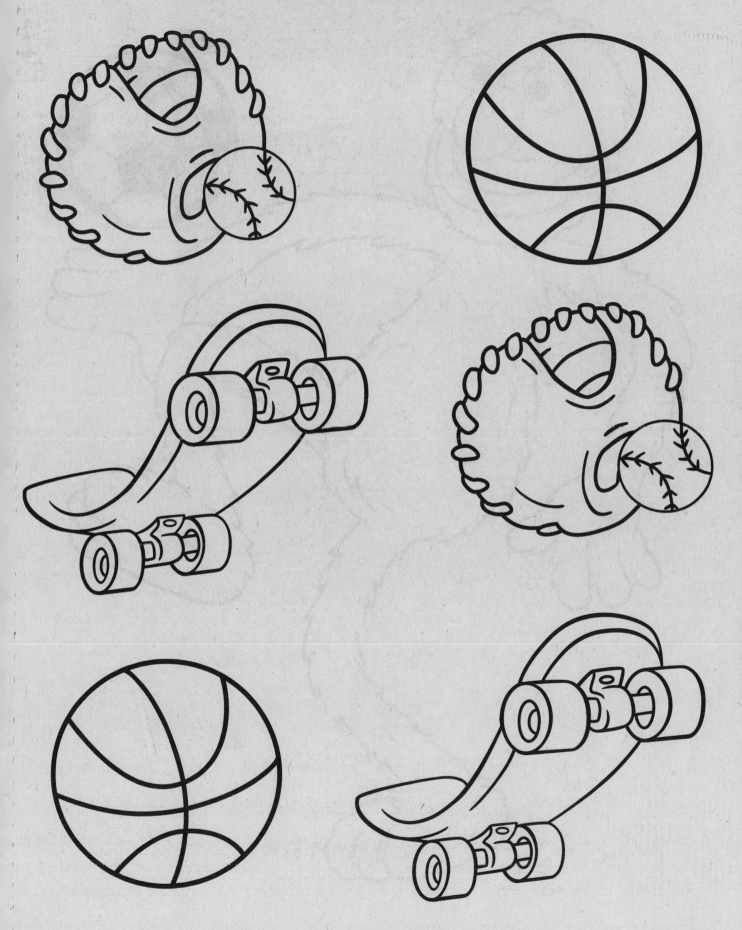

Draw lines between the pictures that match.

Draw lines connecting the pictures that match.

Draw a ladybug by following the numbered pictures.

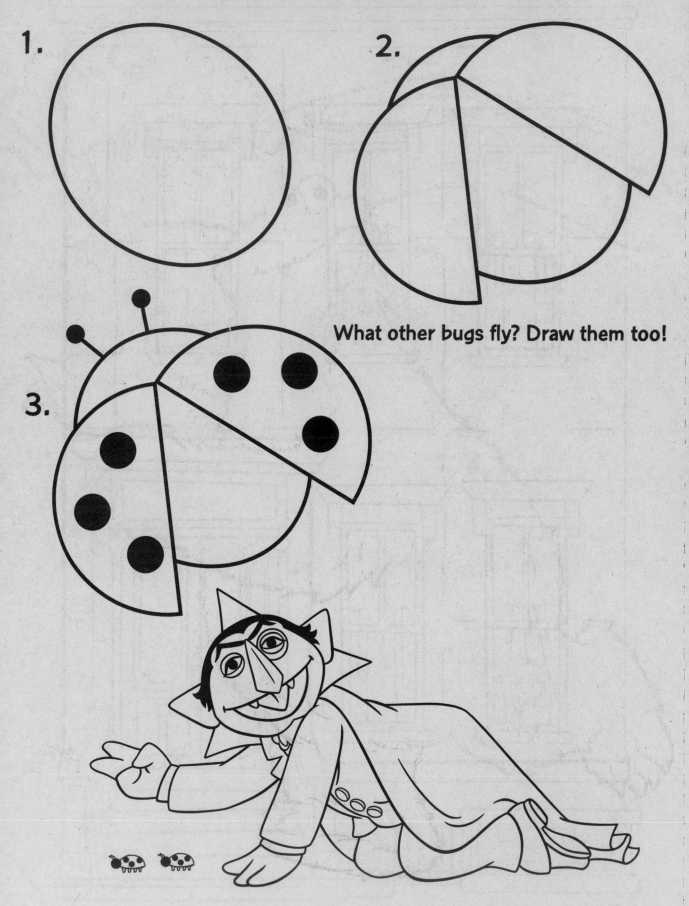

1.

2.

What other bugs fly? Draw them too!

3.

Which present is biggest? Color it red.
Which present is smallest? Color it green.

Color the picture.

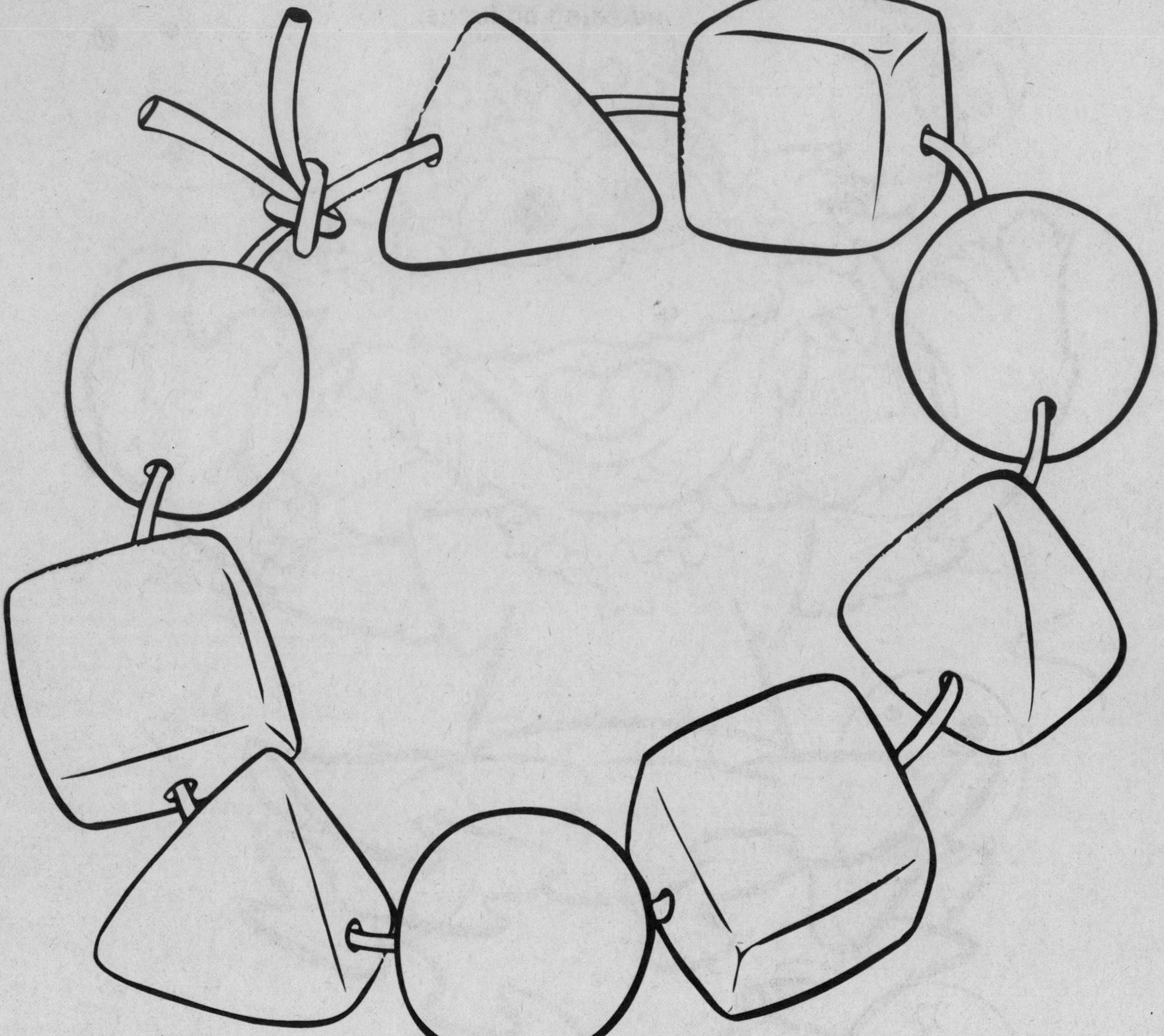

◯ = **red**

△ = **green**

▢ = **blue**

Draw lines connecting the matching balloons.

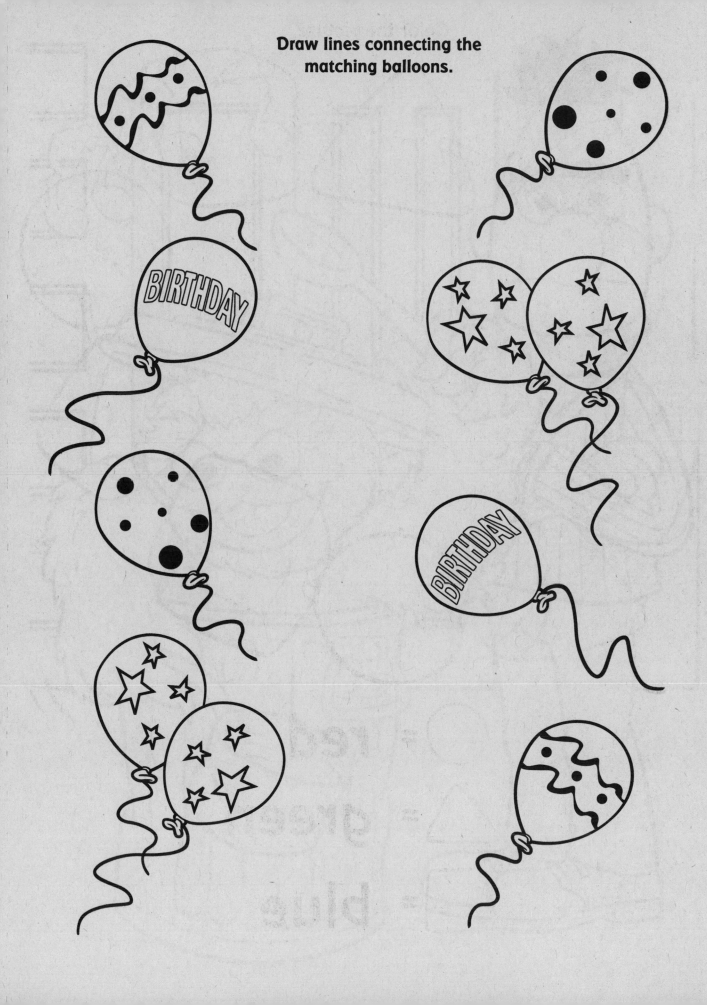

Storytime!
Learning Time!

123
SESAME STREET

For more learning fun with Elmo and friends,
check out the Sesame Street eBookstore at

www.ebooks.sesamestreet.org